Cuisine of Himachal Pradesh: Himachali Dham

Jaswinder Singh

Gaurav Book Centre Pvt. Ltd.

Publisher
Gaurav Book Centre Pvt. Ltd.
4832/24,Prahlad Lane,S-207 Ansari
Road, Daryaganj, Delhi-110002
Ph.: 43570976, 23278261
Email: gauravbookcentre@gmail.com

Edition: 2014

ISBN : 978-93-83316-01-4

Laser Typesetting
JEE-VEE Graphics, Delhi

Price : 195.00

Printer: Vikas Computers, Delhi

CONTENTS

Himachal Pradesh

This is a state in northern India in the spread over 55,670 sq km, it is present on the eastern side of North India bordering Jammu and Kashmir in the North Punjab on the west, Haryana and Uttarakhand in the South and the borders Tibet on the east him means snow in Sanskrit the literal meaning of Himachal Pradesh means in the lap of Himalayas. It was named by a acharaya diwakar datt sharma one of the great scholars of Himachal Pradesh,

historically Himachal has been a group of princely states which included Kannada Bilaspur Rampur sirmour Chamba Mandi . After independence states of Shimla Kannada Kulu lahul aamb una came under Punjab but in 1952 Punjab became a union Territory and further on 25 January 1971 Himachal emerged as the 18th state of India

Himachal is situated in the western Himalayas and has an elevation ranging from 350 m to 7000 m above sea level in two main rivers originating in Himachal are sutlej and beas there is a great Variation in the climatic conditions of Himachal Pradesh due to great variation in topography of the area

the vegetation of the state is dictated by amount of precipitation and altitude south of Himachal has hoped a mostly Himalayan broadleaf forest and subtropical pine forests where as Mr Himalayas comprise mainly of subalpine conifer forest.

Himachal has also been said to be the fruit bowl of the country with orchards scattered all over the state economy is mainly dictated by agriculture which contributes to almost 45% of the state domestic product it is a main source of income and employment in Himachal Pradesh although although the state is deficient in the growth of foodgrains but it compensates with the growth of mushroom chicory seeds hops let's take this and vegetables

Himachal has a very rich heritage in terms of handicrafts and handlooms these include the world-famous pashmina shawls and the famous Kulu headgear and Shawls where as kinnaur is extensively known for its handwoven shawls and woollen cloth

Art and culture due to its epitome during the Kannada Empire when paintings and sculptures gained a lot the day to day diet of Himachal Lees is mainly influenced by local pr the many have dental rice and vegetables the roti is made of flour like wheat maize and is often fermented Himachal is also known for a specific home-made wine in the upper reaches of Himalayan mountain ranges

Himachal Pradesh is not just a state of a single culture or language it is the multicultural multilingual state most commonly spoken languages are hindi, Punjabi, Dogri,,kangari , kinnauri and many multiple dialects each language the many communities that reside in Himachal are mainly Brahmins Rajputs kannets rathis and Kohli's Tamil population also comprises of gaddis kinnars gujjarsand pangwals

Most of the state is Hindu and vegetarian but certain districts are having very different eating habits for example kinnaur lahaul spiti mainly because of tibeatean influence and lesser availability of food products because of the cold in higher reaches of the Himalayas food preservation techniques have also been involved and mastered in the tribal areas. It is noteworthy to see that how the stripes have evolved to not only processed food part also to preserve it for the winter months dried meats alcohol and dry fruits are common ingredients in upper Himalayan food the vegetables eaten mostly comprise off local wild and seasonal products but in recent times with the development of votes and abetted past transportation system the food habits of Himachal Lees has been changing manyfold. Many traditional foods in that were the hallmark of Himachal the food had been lost in time and replaced by easy variable cheek substitutes

KHATTA KADDU

Sr. No.	Ingredients	Quantity
1	Kaddu	350 gms.
2	Mustard Seeds	5gms.
3	Fenugreek	3gms
4	Amchoor Powder	25 gms.
5	Mustard Oil	35 ml.
6	Curry Leaves	2 gms.
7	Heeng	2 gms.
8	Coriander powder	5 gms.
9	Chop green coriander	5 gms.
10	Whole Red Chilly	4 No.s
11	Onion	90 gms.
12	Turmeric	3 gms.
13	Nimbu	Half

METHOD

1. Heat mustard oil in a Karhai and add mustard seeds, fenugreek seeds and curry leaves, sauté a little and add whole red chilly and heeng.
2. Saute till little translucent and add powder spices.
3. Add ½ inch diced Kaddu and add seasoning. Cook for a while till Kaddu becomes tender soft.
4. Add Amchoor powder, sugar, nimbu juice, mix well.
5. Garnish with chopped coriander and serve.

LINGRIAAN DI SALOONI

Sr. No.	Ingredients	Quantity
1	Lingrian	350 gms.
2	Mustard Oil	30 ml.
3	Turmeric	5 gms.
4	Red chilly	5 gms.
5	Salt	To taste
6	Potatoes	150 gms.
7	Garam Masala	5 gms.
8	Onion	120 gms.
9	Jeera powder	5 gms.
10	Coriander Powder	5 gms.
11	Whole Red Chilly	5-6 No.s

METHOD

1. Singe lingri (fern shoots) on open fire and clean with a duster then blanch in hot water.
2. Heat mustard oil in Karhai, add sliced onion and whole red chilly.
3. Add diced potatoes and rest of the dry spices, add water and cook for a while until potatoes are tender.
4. Add lingri to the cooked potatoes, mix well and serve hot with steamed rice with the garnish of chopped coriander.

AALOO MOONGREY

Sr. No.		Ingredients Quantity
1	Moongrey	350 gms.
2	Potatoes	150 gms.
3	Turmeric	5 gms.
4	Red chilly	5 gms.
5	Salt	To taste
6	Mustard Oil	30 ml.
7	Garam Masala	5 gms.
8	Onion	120 gms.
9	Jeera powder	5 gms.
10	Coriander Powder	5 gms.
11	Whole Red Chilly	5-6 No.s

METHOD

1. Cut moongrey into 1-inch batons. Par boil it and keep aside.
2. Heat mustard oil in Karhai, add sliced onion and whole red chilly.
3. Add diced potatoes and rest of the dry spices, add little water and cook for a while until potatoes are tender & water has eventually evaporated.
4. Add moongrey to the cooked potatoes, mix well and serve hot with Chapatti (Phulka) with the garnish of chopped coriander.

BHAEIN DI SABZI

Sr. No.	Ingredients	Quantity
1	Lotus Stem	350 gms.
2	Onion	90 gms.
3	Turmeric	5 gms.
4	Red chilly	5 gms.
5	Salt	To taste
6	Mustard Oil	30 ml.
7	Garam Masala	5 gms.
8	Tomatoes	180 gms.
9	Jeera powder	5 gms.
10	Coriander Powder	5 gms.
11	Garlic chopped	10 gms.
12	Green Coriander	5 gms.
13	Amchoor Powder	5 gms.
14	Ginger chopped	10 gms.

METHOD

1. Cut Lotus stem into 1-inch batons. Bboil it until it is tender and keep aside.
2. Heat mustard oil in Degchi, add chopped ginger and garlic, sauté it for sometime then add chopped onions.
3. Cook it well when it gets golden brown color then add powdered masalas and alongwith chopped tomatoes.
4. Add boiled lotus stems, and cook until everything has melange together properly. Serve it with steamed rice with garnish of chopped coriander.

RAJMAH MADRA

Sr. No.	Ingredients	Quantity
1	Rajmah	350gms
2	Yoghurt	90gms
3	Desi Ghee	30gms
4	Jeera	5gms
5	Cinnamon sticks	2 Nos.
6	Cardamom	2 Nos.
7	Bay Leaves	2 Nos.
8	Cloves	3-4 Nos.
9	Ginger	10gms
10	Garlic	10gms
11	Onions	120gms
12	Makhaney	30gms
13	Turmeric powder	5gms
14	Heeng	2gms
15	Green chillies	2-3 Nos.
16	Red chilli powder	5gms
17	Coriander powder	5gms
18	Jeera powder	5gms
19	Salt	As per the taste
20	Green Coriander	5gms

METHOD

1. Pick, wash and boil Rajmah along with slit green chillies with whole spices, turmeric and heeng till it gets tender and keep aside.
2. Take pan add desi ghee, add cumin then add makhaney after that chopped ginger garlic. Saute it for sometime.
3. Add chopped onions. When it turns golden brown.

Sim the flame and then add yoghurt in it. When it leaves oil to the side, add all the powdered masalas.

4. Add rajmah cook till it Melange well with the gravy
5. Serve it with the garnish of chopped coriander. And have it with the steamed rice.

MAANI

Sr. No.	Ingredients	Quantity
1	Besan	150gms
2	Amchoor	20gms
3	Black horse gram	200gms
4	Mustard oil	45ml
5	Jeera	5gms
6	Cinnamon sticks	2 Nos.
7	Cardamom	2 Nos.
8	Bay Leaves	2 Nos.
9	Cloves	3-4 Nos.
10	Ginger	10gms
11	Garlic	10gms
12	Onions	120gms
13	Curry leaves	2gms
14	Turmeric powder	5gms
15	Heeng	2gms
16	Green chillies	2-3 Nos.
17	Red chilli powder	5gms
18	Coriander powder	5gms
19	Jeera powder	5gms
20	Salt	As per the taste
21	Coriander seeds	3gms
22	Mustard seeds	5gms
23	Fenugreek seeds	3 gms
24	Jaggery	15gms
25	Whole red chilli	3-4 No.

METHOD

1. Pick, wash and boil pre soaked black horse grams along with salt and turmeric.
2. Mix besan with all the powdered masalas together. Add water to make a smooth batter.
3. Take degchi add mustard oil, heat it well then add mustard seeds, coriander seeds, cinnamon sticks, fenugreek seeds, whole red chilli, cardamom, bay leaves, cloves then add heeng in it. Sauté it.
4. Add sliced onion, curry leaves when it turns translucent add water and batter in it. Boil it and then simmer it for 45 minutes.
5. End kadi with amchoor powder, jaggery. Serve it with the steamed rice.

AMBUA

Sr. No.	Ingredients	Quantity
1	Mango (Tapka)	350gms
2	Mustard oil	30ml
3	Cinnamon sticks	2 Nos.
4	Cardamom	2 Nos.
5	Cloves	3-4 Nos.
6	Heeng	2gms
7	Onion	120gms
8	Red chilli powder	5gms
9	Jeera powder	5gms
10	Salt	As per the taste
11	Mustard seeds	5gms
12	Fenugreek seeds	5gms
13	Jaggery	30gms
14	Ginger	5gms

METHOD

1. Pick raw mangoes and wash them well, wrap with the foil and cook on live coal till mangoes become tender.
2. Peal it, scrap out the pulp and coarsely grind it.
3. Take a pan, add oil then add whole spices then add sliced onion and chopped ginger. Cook till it becomes golden brown, and then add red chilli and jeera powder, heeng and pulp. Cook for sometime then add water. Boil it and simmer it for 15-20 minutes. Then add jaggery in it.
4. Serve it with steamed rice.

BANJI

Sr. No.	Ingredients	Quantity
1.	Mango (Raw)	350gms
2.	Onions	240 gms
3.	Black pepper	10gms
4.	Mint	10-12 sprigs
5.	Fenugreek seeds	5gms
6.	Cumin seeds	10gms
7.	Heeng	2gms
8.	Black Salt	5gms
9.	Sugar	250gms
10.	Ginger	2 ltrs
11.	Jiggery/ sugar	450 gms
12.	Water	2 ltrs

METHOD

1. Pick raw mangoes and wash them and peel them. Scrap out the pulp and grate it. Keep aside. Sliced onions add it into the pulp
2. Broil fenugreek seeds, cumin seeds and pepper corns together and then pound them with rolling pin. Keep aside.
3. Take a pan add water then add mangoes and boil it then add sugar, sa3 and pounded masala in it. Simmer it for 30-40 minutes till it gets melange with the water. Refrigerate it for 6 hours.
4. Have it chilled with the garnish of chopped mint.

MALANJI

Sr. No.	Ingredients	Quantity
1	Mango (Raw)	350gms
2	Black pepper	10gms
3	Mint	10-12 sprigs
4	Fenugreek seeds	5gms
5	Cumin seeds	10gms
6	Heeng	2gms
7	Black Salt	10gms
8	Sugar	150gms
9	Water	2 ltrs
10	Oil	30ml
11	Cinnamon sticks	2 Nos.
12	Cardamom	2 Nos.
13	Cloves	3-4 Nos.

METHOD

1. Pick raw mangoes and wash them and peel them. Scrap out the pulp and grate it. Keep aside.
2. Broil fenugreek seeds, cumin seeds and pepper corns together and then pound them with rolling pin. Keep aside.
3. Take a pan, add oil then add sweet spice in it. Add mangoes, sauté it for sometime add water and pounded masala in it. Seasoned it and simmer it for 30-40 minutes till it gets melange with the water.
4. Serve hot with the garnish of chopped mint.

TELIYA MAAH

Sr. No.	Ingredients	Quantity
1	Black gram	400gms
2	Black pepper	2gms
3	Bayleaf	4 nos
4	Coriander seeds	3gms
5	Cumin seeds	3gms
6	Cinnamon	2 noms
7	Cardamom	2nos
8	Black cardamom	2nos
9	Cloves	4 nos
10	Mustard oil	100 ml
11	Green chillies Slit	3 nos
12	Green Coriander	10 gms
13	Turmeric	5 gms
14	Salt	As per taste
15	Red chilli powder	3gms
16	Sliced onions	150gms
17	Water	2ltrs

METHOD

1. Pick wash soak dal keep aside.
2. Take degchi add oil heat it well then add masalas in it. Then add sliced onions sauté it for sometimes add dal and boil it well along with slit green chillies. When water is fully absorbed with the dal remove it from fire serve it with the garnish of green coriander . Have it with steam rice

LAHSUDE

Sr. No.	Ingredients	Quantity
1	Lahsude	350gms
2	Turmeric	10gms
3	Red chilli	5 gms
4	Salt	5gms
5	Cumin seeds	5gms
6	Heeng	2gms
7	Black pepper	5gms
8	Water	For boiling
9	Mustard oil	30 ml

METHOD

1. Boil lahsude till tender remove it refresh them and Sun dry them for six hours.
2. Take deghchi add oil heat it then add sliced onions, green chillies then add lahsude and all the masalas in it
3. Cook for sometime and serve hot with the garnish of green coriander.

BATTAN

Sr. No.	Ingredients	Quantity
1	Besan	225 gms
2	Maize flour	75 gms
3	Saunf	5 gms
4	Ajwain	5 gms
5	Amchoor	15 gms
6	Black pepper	3gms
7	Red chilli	5 gms
8	Mustard oil	For frying
9	Asafoetida	2 gms (dissolved)
10	Ginger	15 gms
11	Arbi leaves (colocasia leaves)	18 to 20 nos.

METHOD

1. Slit arbi leaves from centre in a way to remove its stem, shoot.
2. Wash properly, Keep aside
3. Mix rest of the ingredients to prepare a smooth paste.
4. Apply the paste on the dried leaves placing one after another (Minimum 6)
5. Roll and tie it with the thread.
6. Steam the bricks followed by shallow frying Serve hot with mint sauce

PALDA (TEMPERED CURD)

Sr. No.	Ingredients	Quantity
1	OIL	10 ml
2	Turmeric	3 gms
3	Red chilly	3 gms
4	Garam Masala	3 gms
5	Sugar	15 gms
6	Yoghurt	350 gms
7	Cumin Seeds	5gms
8	Salt	5 gms

METHOD

1. Take Pan, heat oil in it..
2. Add cumin seed to the oil till they crackle.
3. Followed by turmeric, Red chilly & Garam masala powder.
4. Add sugar to the solution.
5. Add a tablespoon of water once the sugar melts.
6. Temper yoghurt wid the prepared mixture.
7. Serve Cold.

NIMKI

Sr. No.	Ingredients	Quantity
1	Raw mango (tapka)	350 gms
2	Oil	30 ml
3	Cumin seeds	10 gms
4	Coriander seeds	5 gms
5	Onion	120 gms
6	Ginger	10 gms
8	Onion seeds (kalonji)	3 gms
9	Jaggery	30 gms
10	Saunf (aniseed)	5 gms
11	Redchilly pwd.	5 gms
12	Salt	To taste

METHOD

1. Peal raw mangoes and slice them keep aside
2. Take a pan add oil heat it well add masalas in it then add slice mangoes cook till tender in the end add jaggery .serve with the chapatti with this

MATAR KE CUTTER

Sr. No.	Ingredients	Quantity
1	Pea pods covers	350 gms
2	Potatoes	350 gms
3	Onion	240 gms
4	Garlic	15 gms
5	Ginger	15 gms
6	Green chillies	10 gms
7	Turmeric	5 gms
8	Garam masala	5 gms
9	Salt	As required
10	Oil	30 ml
11	Cumin	10 gms
12	Green Coriander	15 gms

METHOD

1. Take out pea pods and remove cellulose skin from the covers
2. Blanch them for a minute in hot water and keep aside to self cook
3. In a degchi , heat some oil and add to it cumin seeds till they begin crakling
4. Add chopped onions and cook them till they turn golden brown
5. Add ginger and garlic paste
6. Put in the blanched peas pods cover along with diced potatoes.
7. Top them with red chilli powder,turmeric and garam masala powder in the degchi
8. Steam cook on a slow flame for 15 to 20 mins
9. Garnish with freshly chopped coriander
10. Serve hot with Chapati.

ALOO KI LAUNJI

Sr. No.	Ingredients	Quantity
1	Potatoes	350 gms
2	Mustard seeds	5 gms
3	Oil	15 ml
4	Red chilli powder	5 gms
5	Yoghurt	225 gms
6	Sugar/Jaggery	15 gms
7	Salt	As required
8	Fresh double cream	15 ml
9	Curry leaves	30 to 35 leaves
10	Whole red chilli	5 nos
11	Lemon	1 no.

METHOD

1. Boil potatoes with the skin for few mins and den allow them to self cook for abpout half an hour. (this will not allow potatoes to get mashy)
2. Peel out the skin and cut the potatoes in the dices
3. In a degchi add oil and heat .
4. To the oil add mustard seeds , curry leaves and whole red chilli sticks .
5. Add to it the boiled potatoes seasoned with salt ,turmeric and red chilli powder
6. Turn off the flame after cooking for 5 to 7 mins and allow it to cool for next 10 mins
7. Add to the potatoes , yoghurt and heat gently on a very slow flame .
8. Sprinkle the preparation with lemon and fresh cream.
9. serve this tangy delicacy with puri.

GANDEYALIYAAN

Sr. No.	Ingredients	Quantity
1	Gandeyaliyan	350 gms
2	Tamarind	50 gms
3	Salt	As required
4	Mint	50 gms
5	Sugar	30 gms
6	Black pepper	15 gms
7	Lemon	2 nos

METHOD

1. Boil gandeyalian and peel .
2. Meanwhile prepare a chutney of tamarind and mint leaves using mortar and pestle
3. Season he chutney with salt, black pepper.
4. Add to it lemon juice for tangy flavour
5. Cut thick biteable slices of the tuber and top up with the prepared chutney.

Serve at room temperature

ARBI TALI HUYI (FRIED COLLACASIA)

S. No.	Ingredients	Quantity
1	Arbi (collacasia)	350 gms
2	Onion	240 gms
3	Tomato puree	240 gms
4	Asafoetida	5 gms(dissolved)
5	Whole red chilli	4 nos
6	Turmeric powder	10 gms
7	Kashmiri red chilli powder	10 gms
8	Fresh coriander	15 gms
9	Lemon	2 nos
10	Salt	As required
11	Garam masala	5 gms
12	Aamchoor (dried mango powder)	15 gms
13	Oil	For frying
14	Cumin seeds	5 gms
14	Oil for tempering	45

METHOD

1. Boil arbi ,peel and cut into battons.
2. Heat oil in the degchi .
3. Add cumin seeds followed by chopped onion
4. Cook onion for a while and add tomato puree along wih other above mentioned spices
5. Meanwhile on the other side ;deep fry arbi batons
6. Add deep fried arbi batons to the prepared tempering and top up with fresh lemon drizzle
7. Sprinkle freshly chopped coriander on the top and serve sizzling hot.

BHANGOOR

Sr. No.	Ingredients	Quantity
1	Black horse gram	350 gms
2	Cumin seeds (coarsely pounded)	25 gms
3	Oil	45 ml
4	Salt	As required

METHOD

1. Pick wash and Soak black horse gram in lukewarm water overnight
2. Heat oil in a pan
3. Add cumin seeds to the oil and heat till they begin crakling.
4. Add the black horsegrams and cook covered ...for a duration of 20 mins on a slow flame.
5. Serve with semolina pudding as an accompaniment.

ALOO METHI

Sr. No.	Ingredients	Quantity
1	Fenugreek leaves	A bunch
2	Potatoes	350 gms
3	Onions	120 gms
4	Ginger	30 gms
5	Green chillies	10 gms
6	Turmeric	5 gms
7	Coriander powder	5 gms
8	Jeera powder	5 gms
9	Mustard oil	30 ml
10	Green coriander	10 gms

METHOD

1. Peel and Cut potatoes into 1-inch batons. Par boil it and keep aside. Pluck fenugreek leaves from the sprigs and wash them thoroughly keep aside.
2. Heat mustard oil in Karhai, add sliced onion and whole red chilly.
3. Add diced potatoes and fenugreek leaves together and then add rest of the dry spices, add little water and cook for a while until potatoes are tender & water has eventually evaporated.
4. Serve hot with Chapatti (Phulka) with the garnish of chopped coriander.

BATHU DA SAAG

Sr. No.	Ingredients	Quantity
1	Bathu leaves (amaranth leaves)	1bunch
2	Fenugreek	5 gms
3	Maize flour	90 gms
4	onions	120 gms
5	Garlic	30 gms
6	Green chillies	15 gms
7	Garam masala	5 gms
8	turmeric	5 nos
9	Spinach	1 bunch
10	Mustard oil	90 ml
11	salt	As required

METHOD

1. Wash fresh bathu and spinach leaves (3:1) .
2. Steam cook them together.
3. Use a mortar pestle or traditional ghotta to pound the leaves into rough paste , adding maize flour. simultaneously in little quantity throughout the process .
4. In a separate pan , heat mustard oil till it reaches its burning point and burn the oil steadily for couple of minutes.
5. Let the temp. Of the oil come down followed by the addition of fenugreek into it.
6. Once they begin crackling , add freshly chopped onion garlic and slit green chillies .
7. Temper the pounded bathu with it.
8. Season it well and serve with Maize bread .

RAM TORI

Sr. No.	Ingredients	Quantity
1.	Ridge gourd	350 gms
2.	Double cream	50 ml
3.	Ghee	30 gms
4.	Garam masala	5 gms
5.	Cashew Nuts	15 gms
6.	Salt	As required
7.	Red chilly	5 gms
8.	Cumin seeds	5 gms
9.	Onion	120 gms
10.	Garlic	15 gms
11.	Turmeric	5 gms

METHOD

1. Peel and wash onion , cut them into slices eventually.
2. Cut and chop fresh garlic lobes.
3. In a pan , heat ghee
4. Add cumin seeds and cashews followed by chopped garlic and onions and red chilly powder
5. Cook till onions turn golden brown
6. Add fresh gourd , cut into dices and steam cook for 10 to 12 mins.
7. Season with salt and garam masala for the aromas to rise from the delicacy.
8. Top up with fresh cream.
9. Serve hot with Indian breads.

DANDLAAN D SUBZI

Sr. No.	Ingredients	Quantity
1	Cauliflower stems	350 gms
2	onions	150 gms
3	tomatoes	150 gms
4	ginger	15gms
5	garlic	15 gms
6	Green chillies slit	5 nos
7	lemon	2 nos
8	coriander	10 gms
9	cumin	5 gms
10	Oil	30 ml
11	salt	As required
12	turmeric	5 gms
13	Red chilli powder	5 gms
14	Garam masala	5 gms

METHOD

1. Separate shoots from cauliflower, blanch them and then peel the outer layer from the stems .
2. In a pan , heat some oil.
3. Put cumin seeds followed by chopped ginger and garlic
4. Add sliced onion and cook till the golden brown colour is achieved.
5. Add tomatoes and reduce the mixture to gravy consisteny.
6. Add blanched cauliflower stems.
7. Add turmeric , red chilli powder , garam masala and salt in the end.
8. Serve hot ,drizzling lemon juice to top it up.

KATHAL FRIED

Sr. No.	Ingredients	Quantity
1	kathal(Jack fruit)	350gms
2	Onions	240 gms
3	Ginger	15 gms
4	Garlic	15 gms
5	Deghi Red chilly	10 gms
6	Amchoor	15 gms
7	Turmeric	5 gms
8	Salt	As required
9	Coriander	5 gms
10	Cumin	5 gm
11	Green coriander	15 gms
12	Green chillies chopped	3 nos
13	Oil	50 ml

METHOD

1 Peel jackfruit by applying oil to the hands otherwise itching will start because it contains itching liquid in it.

2 Cut into 2 inches slices and then deep fry it

3 Mix all dried powdered masalas together

4 Take a pan add oil in it heat it well add cumin seeds then add ginger garlic and onions sauté till it gets golden brown colour then add fried jack fruit in it sprinkle masala over it mix it well serve with the garnish of green coriander

SHALGAM DI SUBJI

Sr. No.	Ingredients	Quantity
1	Shalgam (turnips)	350 gms
2	Desi ghee	60 gms
3	Onions	120 gms
4	Green chillies	10 gms
5	ginger	10 gms
6	garlic	10 gms
7	Chopped coriander	15 gms
8	Turmeric	5 gms
9	Lemon	2 nos
10	Garam masala	5 gms
11	Cumin	5 gms
12	Cumin powder	5 gms
13	Coriander powder	5 gms
14	Salt	As required

METHOD

1 Wash peel and cut turnips into small dices keep aside

2 Take deghchi add desi ghee add cumin crackle it well then add ginger and garlic saute it for sometimes add chopped onions then green chillies and add turnip by adding little water cook them with the lid on .

3 Season vegetable and add rest of the ingredients serve with hot with chapatti.

POORE

Sr. No.	Ingredients	Quantity
1	Flour	225 gms
2	Meethi Saunf (Aniseeds)	15 gms
3	Sugar	75 gms
4	Desi ghee	For frying
5	Water for making batter	125 ml
7	Yeast	5 gms

METHOD

1. Make a batter from flour then add aniseeds and sugar along with yeast keep aside for Two hours.
2. Take a tawa heat it well then add desi ghee then pour batter over it shape them into disc with bowl griddled it from both sides serve with kheer.

Manday

Sr. No.	Ingredients	Quantity
1	flour	500
2	Mustard oil	60 ml
3	Salt	10 gms
4	Milk	120 ml
5	water	240 ml

METHOD

1. Knead a soft dough with flour and rest of the ingredients. Keep aside for 30mins.
2. Make roundals from the dough of nearly 60 gms.
3. Roll it and Flatten them into a 10 inches diameter disc.
4. Griddle it well on spherical tawa.
5. Have it hot with vegetables prepration.

MITHA ROT

Sr. No.	Ingredients	Quantity
1	Wheat Flour	350 gms
2	Saunf	15 gms
3	Ghee	50 gms
4	Raisins	15 gms
5	Cashew Nuts (finely chopped)	30 gms
6	Sugar/Jaggery	75 gms
7	water	155 ml
8	milk	25 ml

METHOD

1. Add all the ingredients in Dry Flour.
2. Prepare a smooth dough and keep it to rest for atleast half n hour.
3. Prepare chapatti shaped roundels of the above prepared dough.
4. Shallow fry on a very slow flame .

BEDMI ROTI

	Ingredients	Quantity
1.	Maize Flour	350 gms
2.	Methi leaves fresh	Half bunch leaves
3.	Raddish	200 gms
4.	Ghee	35 gms
5.	Salt	As required
6.	Ajwain	5 gms
7.	Water	180 ml

METHOD

1. Shred raddish in a bowl add little salt in it and keep aside for sometime. then squeeze out the excess water.
2. Take small quantity of maize flour in a small bowl
3. Add all the ingredients in the bowl to prepare the dough
4. Add small amounts of water if needed
5. Prepare round roti's and heat on the griddle on a slow flame.
6. Top up the roti with ghee or white butter
7. Serve with pickle and tea.

MEETHE BABRU

Sr. No.	Ingredients	Quantity
1	Wheat flour	225 gms
2	Desi ghee (clarified butter)	For frying
3	Saunf	15 gms
4	Curd	30 ml
5	Sliced Coconut (thuthi)	30 gms
6	Sugar/Jaggery	75 gms
7	Raisins	15 gms
8	water	125 ml

METHOD

1. Add curd and water to wheat flour along with jaggery to make a thick batter .
2. Keep the dough in sunlight for couple of hours to ferment
3. Add saunf ,raisins.
4. Heat Desi ghee for frying dumpling in deep pan.
5. Form dumplings of the batter and deep fry till brown.
6. Served at room temperature and has very long shelf life.

MATHI

Sr. No.	Ingredients	Quantity
1	Wheat Flour	350 gms
2	Ajwain	15 gms
3	Ghee	50 ml
4	Salt	10 gms
5	Oil	For frying

METHOD

Mathi is one of the variety of north Indian puri but hard and has a very long shelf life)

1. Give moin to the flour by adding ghee in it and make a hard dough by adding rest of the ingredients.
2. Heat oil in a degchi.
3. Take out the roundals from the dough flatten them into 5 inches disc.
4. Deep fry .
5. Served in the main course with different preparations.

MUNTANJNA

Sr. No.	Ingredients	Quantity
1	Budana	225 gms
2	Meethi Saunf (Aniseeds)	25 gms
3	Sugar syrup (double thread)	225 gms
4	Desi ghee	50gms
5	Cashews	30 gms
6	Almonds	30 gms
7	Raisins	30 gms
8	Makhana	30 gms
9	Dried apples	30 gms
10	Dried dates	30 gms
11	Green cardamom	10 nos
12	Big cardamom	5 nos
13	Cloves	5 nos
14	Dried Coconut sliced	30 gms
15	Melon seeds	15 gms
16	Saffron	2 gms

Only dessert course in typical himachli dham have it with rice

Method

1 heat ghee add all the dried fruits in it cook till they turns a little colour then add sugar syrup which is flavoured with saffron .

2 In the end add budana in it serve hot with rice or you can have it as it is.

MITTHA KADDU

Sr. No.	Ingredients	Quantity
1	Kaddu (Sweet &aged)	350 gms.
2	Mithi Saunf	10 gms.
3	Grated Coconut	90 gms.
4	Cashew nuts	30 gms.
5	Almonds	30 gms.
6	Desi ghee	125 gms.
7	Kishmish (Raisins)	15 gms.
8	Jaggery	120 gms.
9	Green cardamom (powdered)	5 gms.

METHOD

1. Heat Desi ghee in Karhai add mithi saunf, cashew nut, almond, raisins. Cook for a while.
2. Add grated coconut alongwith grated Kaddu.
3. When Kaddu becomes soft, add jiggery and green cardamom powder.
4. Serve with the garnish of dry nuts.